An ATC & Drum Theatre Plymouth Production

The Golden Dragon

by Roland Schimmelpfennig

translated by David Tushingham

The World premiere of *The Golden Dragon*
was staged at the Burgtheater, Vienna on 5 September 2009,
directed by Roland Schimmelpfennig.

The English language premiere of *The Golden Dragon* took place
at the Drum Theatre Plymouth on 12 May 2011.

ATC's licence to present Roland Schimmelpfennig's play *The Golden Dragon*
is granted by arrangement with Rosica Colin Limited, London, working in
conjunction with S Fischer Verlag Frankfurt am Main.

**GOETHE
INSTITUT**

T0347990

Supported by
**ARTS COUNCIL
ENGLAND**

The Golden Dragon

by Roland Schimmelpfennig
translated by David Tushingham

CAST

David Beames	**A Man Over 60**
Adam Best	**A Young Man**
Ann Firbank	**A Woman Over 60**
Kathryn O'Reilly	**A Young Woman**
Jack Tarlton	**A Man**

CREATIVE TEAM

Director	Ramin Gray
Aesthetic Inspiration	Johannes Schütz
Associate Designer	Natasha Piper
Lighting Designer	Stephen Andrews
Musical Arrangement	Zenghui Qiu
Sound Designer	Alexander Caplen
Casting Director	Julia Horan CDG
Assistant Director	Nick Bruckman
Company Stage Manager	Jess Banks
Production Manager	Nick Soper
Drum Theatre Technician	Matt Hoyle
Costume Supervisor	Dina Hall
Wardrobe Mistress	Cheryl Hill
Set, Props and Costumes	TR2, Theatre Royal Plymouth Production Centre

ROLAND SCHIMMELPFENNIG - Writer

Roland Schimmelpfennig was born in Göttingen in 1967. After a prolonged stay in Istanbul as a journalist, he studied stage direction at the Otto-Falkenberg-School in Munich. Following his studies he became assistant director at the Kammerspiele Munich, and from 1995 onwards he was a member of the artistic direction of the theatre. He has been working as a freelance author since 1996. In 1998 he went to the United States for a year and there primarily worked as a translator. Schimmelpfennig worked as dramaturg at the Schaubühne Berlin from 1999 to 2001. In the season of 2001/2002 he was author-in-residence at the Schauspielhaus in Hamburg. Since 2000 he has been commissioned to write plays for the State Theatres in Stuttgart and Hannover, the Schauspielhaus Hamburg, the Burgtheater Vienna, the Schauspielhaus Zurich, the German Theatre Berlin and others. In 2010, Schimmelpfennig was awarded the Mühlheimer Dramatists Award for *The Golden Dragon*. Schimmelpfennig also received the highest Playwriting Award in Germany, the Else-Lasker-Schüler-Prize, to honour his entire *oeuvre*. He lives in Berlin.

"Roland Schimmelpfennig is the leading German dramatist."
Frankfurter Rundschau

DAVID BEAMES – A Man over 60

Training: Bristol Old Vic Theatre School 1969/71.

Theatre credits include: *Henry V, Henry VI Parts 1, 2 & 3, Richard III, Henry VIII, Camino Real, Son of Man, The Broken Heart, The Spanish Tragedy, Zenobia, The Wives' Excuse, Les Enfants du Paradis* (Royal Shakespeare Company); *Fuente Ovejuna, Peer Gynt, Her Naked Skin, The Father, Danton's Death* (Royal National Theatre); *Richard III* (Royal National Theatre/ American Tour); *Called to Account, The Bloody Sunday Inquiry, Justifying War: Scenes from the Hutton Inquiry* (Tricycle Theatre); *Borderline, A Colder Climate, The Grace of Mary Traverse, Submariners* (Royal Court Theatre); *Dancing Attendance, Miss Firecracker Contest* (Bush Theatre); *Holy Days* (Soho Poly); *A Christmas Carol* (Manchester Library); *Comedians* (Old Vic/ UK Tour; Many Plays 1975/77 Nottingham Playhouse Co); *The Price, Love for Love, All Things Bright and Beautiful, Joseph's Dreamcoat* (Liverpool Playhouse Theatre); *Roots* (Royal Exchange Theatre, Manchester); *Festen* (Birmingham Rep/ UK Tour); *Twelfth Night, Richard II, Who's Afraid Of Virginia Woolf?* (Bristol Old Vic); *Macbeth* (Albery Theatre); *Feelgood* (Out of Joint/ Garrick Theatre); *Our Country's Good* (Out of Joint/ Young Vic/ International Tour); *A Month In The Country* (Salisbury Playhouse); *Duchess of Malfi* (Oxford Playhouse); *Spotted Dick* (Watford Palace); *The Hinge of The World,* (Yvonne Arnaud Theatre, Guildford); *Too True to be Good* (Shared Experience); *Pride and Prejudice* (Bath Theatre Royal/ UK Tour). Film credits include: *McVicar, Dark Water, Radio On.* Radio credits include: many plays for BBC Manchester. Television credits include: *Midsomer Murders, A Touch of Frost, Fair Stood the Wind for France, Miss Marple, Destiny, Justifying War: Scenes from the Hutton Enquiry, The Rainbow,*

Boon, Casualty, Cop Out, Crimesquad, For the Greater Good, Holby City, Maelstrom, Pie in the Sky, Submariners, Rumpole of the Bailey, School for Clowns, The Bill, Doctors, Emmerdale.

ADAM BEST – A Young Man

Training: Royal Welsh College of Music & Drama.

Theatre credits include: *Northern Star* (Finborough Theatre); Vincent in *Pieces of Vincent* (Arcola Theatre); Mason in *Journey's End* (UK Tour); Man in *On A Starless Night* (Box of Tricks); Remco in *Truckstop* (Eastern Angels/Company of Angels); Joseph in *By the Bog of Cats* (Wyndham's Theatre). TV and Film Credits include: Ben in *Blooded* (Magma Pictures); Charlie Winter in *Silent Witness* (BBC Television); Quinn in *Waking the Dead* (BBC TV); Connor Deegen in *The Bill* (Talkback Thames); Patrick in *The Catherine Tate Show* (Tiger Aspect); Series Regular Matt Parker in *Holby City* (BBC Television). Other credits: *John Walker's Blues* (BBC Radio); *Dogs* - Rehearsed Reading (Hampstead Theatre); *Leopoldville* - Rehearsed Reading (Box of Tricks); *Ismene* - Rehearsed Reading (Theatre503).

ANN FIRBANK – A Woman Over 60

Training: Old Vic Theatre School/RADA.

ATC theatre credits include: *Celestina, Ion, The Belle Vue, Orpheus.* Other theatre credits include: *Three Sisters, An Ideal Husband, Separate Tables, Habitat, The Candidate* (Manchester Royal Exchange); *An Argument About Sex* (Tramway/Traverse Theatre); *King Arthur* (Arcola); *Ana in Love* (Hackney Empire); *Only the Lonely* (Birmingham Rep); *Macbeth* (Almeida); *Beckett* (Theatre Royal Haymarket); *Three Woman* (Riverside Studios); *Wonderful Beast, Maps of Desire* (Southwark Playhouse); *Les Liaisons Dangereuses* (Liverpool Playhouse); *Henry V, The Comedy of Errors* (RSC); *Macbeth, Postcards from Rome, A Working Woman, Tess of the D'Urbervilles* (West Yorkshire Playhouse); *Much Ado About Nothing* (Cheek by Jowl); *Hedda Gabler* (English Touring Theatre); *The Invisible Woman*, directed by Ramin Gray (Gate Theatre); *The House of Mirth* (Cambridge Theatre Company); *Macbeth* (Oxford Stage Company); *A Doll's House* (Royal Lyceum Theatre, Edinburgh); *The Winter's Tale, Romeo and Juliet* (Actor – USA university tours); *Mary Stuart* (BAC); *God Say Amen* (ESC); *Twelfth Night, Anthony and Cleopatra* (Stratford Ontario); *The Old Devils* (Theatr Clwyd); *A Handful of Dust* (Shared Experience); *High Society* (Victoria Palace Theatre); *The Passion, Julius Caesar* (National Theatre), worldwide tours of *The Hollow Crown* (RSC) and many wonderful Beast productions (London/Suffolk/Jaipur). Television credits include: *Midsomer Murders, Kingdom, Eastenders, Elizabeth I, Doctors, 10th Kingdom, An Evil Streak, Kavanagh QC, Heartbeat, Animal Ark, Surgical, Boon, Heart of the Country, Growing Rich, Poirot, The Good Guys, Motherlove, Hotel Du Lac, Flesh and Blood, Lillie, The Nearly*

Man, Crown Court and *Persuasion*. Film credits include: *Esther Khan, Anna and the King, Strapless, Lionheart, A Passage to India, The Magic Box, Sunday Bloody Sunday, A Severed Head, Accident, The Servant, Asylum, Carry on Nurse* and many short films.

KATHRYN O'REILLY – A Young Woman

Training: Kathryn graduated from LAMDA in 2008.

Theatre credits include: For Out of Joint, *Andersen's English* (Hampstead Theatre), *Mixed Up North* (Wilton's Music Hall) both directed by Max Stafford-Clark; *A Christmas Carol* (Trafalgar Studios); *Love on the Tracks* (Soho Theatre Studio); *Oedipus* (National Tour Inc Sheffield Crucible). Film credits include: *Random, Zebra Crossing*. Television credits include: *Lewis V, The Bill, Rough Justice*. Rehearsed reading credits include: *Write Up* – directed by Ben Woolf (Donmar Warehouse); *Lullabye Burn* – directed by Dominic Cooke (Royal Court); *My Heart's a Suitcase* – directed by Max Stafford-Clark (Royal Court); *Klink Klank Echoes* – directed by Hannah Eidinow (Tristan Bates).

JACK TARLTON – A Man

Training: London Academy of Music and Dramatic Art.

Theatre credits include: *Beasts and Beauties* (Hampstead Theatre & Bristol Old Vic); *What Every Woman Knows* (Finborough Theatre); For Propeller - *The Merchant of Venice, A Midsummer Night's Dream* (Liverpool Playhouse, The Rose, The Watermill, Brooklyn Academy of Music, Metropolitan Arts Space, Tokyo & international tour), *The Taming of the Shrew, Twelfth Night* (The Old Vic, The Watermill, RSC Complete Works Festival, Brooklyn Academy of Music & international tour); *The Deep Blue Sea* (Theatre Royal Bath Productions – Vaudeville Theatre & national tour); *The Sexual Neuroses of Our Parents* (The Gate); *She Stoops to Conquer* (Manchester Royal Exchange); *Coram Boy, Once in a Lifetime* (National Theatre), *The Man Who* (Orange Tree); *Gagarin Way* (Primecut); *Romeo and Juliet* (Chichester Festival Theatre); *Howie the Rookie* (Fourth Road); *Afore Night Come* (Young Vic); *An Inspector Calls* (Garrick Theatre); *A Month in the Country, Troilus and Cressida* (Royal Shakespeare Company). Film credits include: *The Unscarred*. Television credits includes: *Doctors, The Golden Hour, Dead Ringers, Doctor Who, The Genius of Mozart, Swivel on the Tip, Hearts and Bones, Life Support, Wings of Angels, The Cater Street Hangman*. Radio credits include: *The Teahouse Detective – The Edinburgh Mystery*.

DAVID TUSHINGHAM – Translator

David has translated numerous plays by Roland Schimmelpfennig including *Arabian Night* (ATC) and *The Woman Before* (Royal Court). Other translations include: *Jeff Koons* (ATC); *Karate Billy Comes Home, Waiting Room Germany, Stranger's House, Mr Kolpert* (all Royal Court Theatre); *State of Emergency* (Gate); *Innocence* (Arcola). He has worked as a dramaturg for numerous high-profile European institutions including LINZ09 European Capital of Culture, the Wiener Festwochen, National Theatre London, Theater der Welt and the Ruhrtriennale, for whom he has commissioned and collaborated with remarkable artists on new works across a wide range of performance disciplines. He is the author of numerous books, articles and workshops and currently lectures at the London College of Fashion. From Autumn 2011 he will be artistic advisor to Düsseldorfer Schauspielhaus and the theatre programme of the Salzburger Festspiele.

RAMIN GRAY – Director

Ramin is ATC's new Artistic Director. *The Golden Dragon* is his first production for the company.

Previously, he was International Associate (2000-05), then Associate Director (2005-09) at the Royal Court Theatre where he directed many world or British premieres by playwrights including Simon Stephens' *Motortown* (also Wiener Festwochen), Marius von Mayenburg's *The Ugly One* and *The Stone*, Mark Ravenhill's *Over There* (also Schaubühne, Berlin), the Presnyakov Brothers' *Terrorism*, Vassily Sigarev's *Ladybird*, Juan Mayorga's *Way to Heaven*, David Watson's *Just a Bloke*, Marina Carr's *Woman With Scarecrow* and Roland Schimmelpfennig's *Push Up*.

Other credits include David Greig's *The American Pilot* and Leo Butler's *I'll Be The Devil* for the Royal Shakespeare Company, co-direction with Max Stafford-Clark of Alastair Beaton's *King Of Hearts* for Out of Joint/Hampstead as well as the first UK production of a Jon Fosse play, *The Child* at the Gate.

In the German-speaking theatre he has directed productions of Simon Stephens *On The Shore of the Wide World* (Karl Skraup Prize, Volkstheater Wien) and *Harper Reagan* (Deutsche Schauspielhaus Hamburg and Salzburg Festspiele) as well as Dennis Kelly's *Orphans* (Schauspielhaus Wien). In Russia, his production of *The Ugly One* is in the repertoire at Praktika, Moscow (Best Director Textura Festival Perm). He has also directed three plays by Gregory Motton in Paris, Liverpool and London.

Opera credits include the European premiere of *Bliss* by Brett Dean and Benjamin Britten's *Death in Venice* at Hamburg's Staatsoper and Theater an der Wien.

NATASHA PIPER – Associate Designer

Natasha joined ATC as Associate Designer in April 2011. Growing up in Brussels to designer parents, she was exposed to the creative world from a young age. She was soon enticed by London life where she moved in 2006 to enroll at Wimbledon College of Art, before training in stage design at Central School of Speech and Drama, graduating in 2010.

Natasha's contribution to stage design includes costumes for devised piece *The Ship* directed by Nick Philippou (East 15), costumes for the period musical *The Mystery of Edwin Drood* (CSSD '10), *The Silver Tree* with Avant Garde dance company (Paradise Gardens festival 2009). Assisting includes four productions for High Tide Festival (Suffolk and touring), BBC 3's *Psychoville, Get Santa!* (Royal Court), *A Little Neck* with Goat & Monkey (Hampton Court) amongst others.

STEPHEN ANDREWS – Lighting Designer

Credits as Associate Lighting Designer include: *Seagull* (Royal Court Production, Broadway); *Enron* (Royal Court and Headlong Production, West End); *Jerusalem* (Royal Court Production, West End); *Clybourne Park* (Royal Court Production, West End).

ZENGHUI QIU – Musical Arrangement

Zenghui Qiu is a highly versatile Chinese musician, with over 20 years experience playing a wide range of Chinese music, including Beijing Opera, Chinese classical music and folk music. She is a graduate in instrumental music from the Tianjin Opera School and the China National Beijing Opera College. After graduation she performed in the National Beijing Opera Company for nearly ten years, and worked for the re-established Mei Lanfang Opera Troupe from 1996 to 1999.

Since moving to Britain in 1999, she has performed on many occasions, at venues including the Queen Elizabeth Hall and Birmingham Symphony Hall, and World Music festivals including WOMEX 2006 (Spain) and WOMAD 2007 (UK). She has taught at SOAS, University of London, and has given workshops at numerous schools and other organisations around the country. She has also recorded music for CD and film.

In addition to her expert understanding of Beijing Opera, Zenghui plays a wide variety of Chinese instruments, including jinghu (bamboo fiddle), erhu (two-string Chinese fiddle), yueqin (moon lute), dizi (bamboo flute), suona (Chinese oboe), hulu si (gourd pipe), guzheng (Chinese zither), zhongruan (bass lute), and percussion.

Zenghui is currently performing with Yellow Earth theatre in their touring show *Why the Lion Danced*.

ALEXANDER CAPLEN – Sound Designer

Alex is Deputy Head of Sound at The Royal Court Theatre and an Associate Artist (Sound) at ATC.

Sound design credits include: *Ogres* (Tristan Bates); *Wanderlust* (Royal Court); *It's About Time* (Nabokov), *The Love for Three Oranges, Tosca* (Grange Park Opera); *Mine, Ten Tiny Toes, War and Peace* (Shared Experience); *Over There* (Royal Court & Schaubühne Berlin); *Stephen and the Sexy Partridge* (Old Red Lion/ Trafalgar Studios); *Peter Pan, Holes, Duck Variations* (UK Tour); *The Wizard of Oz, The Entertainer* (Nuffield Theatre); *Imogen* (Oval House/ Tour). Credits as sound operator/engineer include: *Wig Out!, Rhinoceros, The Arsonists, Free Outgoing, Now or Later, Gone Too Far, The Pain & The Itch* (Royal Court); *Edinburgh Military Tattoo 2009 & 2010*; *Brontë, Kindertransport* (Shared Experience); *Blood Brothers* (International tour); *Ballroom* (UK tour). Other work includes large-scale music touring as a Front of House mix engineer.

JULIA HORAN CDG – Casting Director

Theatre credits include: *Wastwater; The Heretic; Get Santa!; Kin; Red Bud; Tribes; Clybourne Park; Wanderlust; Spur of the Moment; Sucker Punch; Ingredient X; The Force of Change; Yardgal* (Royal Court); *The Knot of the Heart; Through a Glass Darkly; Measure for Measure; When the Rain Stops Falling; In a Dark Dark House; The Homecoming; Nocturne; Awake and Sing, Dying for It; Out of the Fog* (Almeida); *Glass Menagerie; Joe Turner's Come and Gone; Annie Get Your Gun; In The Red and Brown Water; Lost Highway; The Good Soul of Szechuan; Tintin; The Skin of our Teeth; Hobson's Choice; The Daughter-in-law; Homebody Kabul; A Raisin in the Sun; Six Characters Looking for an Author* (Young Vic); *Clybourne Park; Arcadia; Swimming with Sharks; As You Like It; Antarctica; The Weir* (West End); *A Brief History of Helen of Troy, Bad Jazz* (ATC); *Six Characters in Search of an Author* (Chichester Festival Theatre/ West End/ Sydney Festival); *pool (no water)* (Frantic Assembly); *Gaddafi - A Living Myth* (English National Opera); *Three Sisters on Hope Street; Anna in the Tropics; Yellowman* (Hampstead Theatre); *Othello* (Cheek by Jowl); *The Girl on the Sofa* (Edinburgh International Festival/ Schaubühne Theatre, Berlin). Television credits include: *Adha Cup; Parliamo Glasgow; Harvest; The Verdict; The Bill; The Badness of King George IV*.

NICK BRUCKMAN – Assistant Director

Trained at Drama Centre London with a full VandenEnde Foundation scholarship. Since graduating, he continued training at Living Pictures, with directors including Ian Rickson, Katie Mitchell, Roxanna Silbert and Dominic Cooke, worked on development weeks at the Young Vic, and as a trainee director at the Maxim Gorki Theater Berlin. He was shortlisted for the JMK Award in 2010, and selected for the Lincoln Center Directors Lab 2011 in New York.

Directing credits include: *Destination Jonestown* (Theatre Royal Stratford East, development workshops); *Miss Julie* (Arcola Theatre, also translator); *Communication Breakdown* (Theatre503, RWR); *Sister Of* (Nursery Festival, Nottingham Playhouse, Bike Shed Theatre Exeter, also co-translator); *Hot Air* (Edinburgh Fringe Festival). Assisting credits include: *Ich Werde Hier Sein Im Sonnenschein Und Im Schatten* – directed by Armin Petras (Staatstheater Stuttgart/ Maxim Gorki Theater Berlin); *Take Away* – directed by Kerry Michael (Theatre Royal Stratford East, workshop); *League of Youth* – directed by Giles Croft (Nottingham Playhouse, development).

JESS BANKS – Company Stage Manager

Trained in Stage Management at the Royal Welsh College of Music and Drama. Theatre credits include: *Shoes* (Sadler's Wells); *Cinderella, Sleeping Beauty, Aladdin* (Cheltenham Everyman); *Pleasure's Progress* (Royal Opera House); *Chicago* (Aberystwyth Arts Centre); *The Marriage of Figaro, A Midsummer Night's Dream, Don Pasquale* (English Touring Opera); *Quadrophenia* (Kenny Wax Ltd); *Vagina Monologues, Debbie Does Dallas* (Mark Goucher Ltd); *The 39 Steps* (Fiery Angel, UK Tour).

ATC challenges and inspires a wide-range of audiences by touring ambitious contemporary theatre with a strong international focus. Our work is made by bringing together emerging and established artists from many spheres and backgrounds. Based in East London but working closely with regional, national and international partners, ATC takes excellent theatre everywhere.

Since 1980 we've toured throughout England and beyond, introducing cutting-edge theatre to people who might not otherwise have the chance to experience it. In the next four years, we'll evolve a leaner, greener aesthetic, minimizing our carbon footprint while maximising our contact with audiences.

ATC has maintained a consistently cosmopolitan outlook. Now, by forging an innovative series of national and international collaborations, we'll leverage the company's resources both artistically and financially, reducing our financial dependence on ACE while extending our artistic reach.

ATC is flexible, nimble in its response to new inputs and steadfast in its quest to create and deliver genuinely innovative theatre practice. With our proven track record, ATC will continue to ensure we reach the broadest possible audiences.

Artistic Director: Ramin Gray
Executive Director: Nick Williams
Administrator & Events Manager: Kendall O'Neill
Spin Off Coordinator: Ben Assefa-Folivi
Collaborative Doctorate*: Christine Twite
Press Agent: David Burns
Administrative Intern: Svenja Fischer

*In partnership with Queen Mary University of London

ATC
The Tab Centre, 3 Godfrey Place,
London E2 7NT
T: +44 (0) 20 7033 7360
www.atctheatre.com / atc@atctheatre.com

SPIN OFF runs throughout ATC's process and performances. We aim to open our work to the audience from before the show starts to after they've seen it, and give opportunities for people to get involved and participate. We hope that SPIN OFF will contextualise our work and make it more accessible as it acts as a forum for discussion and involvement around the themes and issues that our productions raise.

A new element of this is our Open Rehearsal process – piloted on *The Golden Dragon* giving unprecedented access to Ramin Gray's rehearsal room. Through regular video podcasts, we've introduced the processes and the people that have gone into making the show and our innovative *Mystery Guest* slot allows anyone who is interested to tweet us, for a chance to visit the rehearsal room as an observer. We intend on developing this programme in future to give the richest possible engagement with ATC's work.

ACT@ATC

ACT@ATC is aimed specifically at young people under 26 in our local Hackney and Tower Hamlets area. It follows the same ethos as our SPIN OFF programme by nurturing and supporting young talent to make theatre. ACT@ATC offers a variety of workshops and events throughout the year ranging from playwriting and acting workshops to performances. The group has written and performed its own work as well as participating in bigger projects including the development of a new play for NT Connections in 2012 and recording an original radio drama for BBC London.

All ACT@ATC events are free for our young people to take part in. We also run a bi-monthly ACT@ATC e-newsletter keeping our group up to date on our current projects and other related opportunities.

To get involved, email us at spinoff@atctheatre.com or check our website for info on our upcoming projects.

DRUM THEATRE

PLYMOUTH THEATRES

"At Plymouth they are maximising the potential of those who could be the great theatre-makers of tomorrow...You only have to look around British Theatre to see the Drum's fingerprints everywhere."
THE GUARDIAN

The Drum Theatre produces and presents new plays. As part of the Theatre Royal Plymouth we have built a national reputation for the quality of our programme and innovative work, winning the Peter Brook Empty Space Award in 2007. In addition to our own commissioned productions, we sometimes collaborate with other leading theatre companies like ATC including, most recently, Told by an Idiot, Paines Plough, the Royal Court Theatre, Frantic Assembly and the Belgian company, Ontroerend Goed.

"Now, under Simon Stokes, Plymouth has become a magnet for talent."
THE OBSERVER

In 2009 we had major success with a new 'horror' comedy, *Grand Guignol* by Carl Grose and co-produced a new experimental work, *Under the Influence*, with Ontroerend Goed. 2010 saw us collaborate with them again on *Teenage Riot* which played Plymouth and Ghent ahead of the Edinburgh Festival and subsequent European tour. We also co-produced Sarah Ruhl's *Eurydice* with ATC and DC Moore's award-winning *The Empire* with the Royal Court Theatre. Our recent co-productions of Mike Bartlett's *Love, Love, Love* with Paines Plough and *And The Horse You Rode In On* with Told by an Idiot are now both touring nationally. Our production of *Chekhov in Hell* by Dan Rebellato transferred to London's Soho Theatre in April 2011.

The Theatre Royal's Young Company and People's Company, both based at TR2, also perform in the Drum Theatre. TR2, our production and education centre, is a truly unique facility. This architecturally award-winning building contains unrivalled set, costume, prop-making and rehearsal facilities. Some of our most important and vigorous work is carried out here by our Creative Learning team, who provide one of the most comprehensive education and outreach programmes in the UK.

DRUM THEATRE

PLYMOUTH THEATRES

"What would British Theatre do without the Drum?"
THE GUARDIAN

Chairman - **Sir Michael Lickiss**
Chief Executive - **Adrian Vinken OBE**
Artistic Director - **Simon Stokes**
Production & Technical Director - **David Miller**
Finance Director - **Paul James**
Marketing & Sales Director - **Marianne Locatori**
Creative Learning Director - **Victoria Allen**
Theatre Manager - **Jack Mellor**
Artistic Associate - **David Prescott**
Technical Coordinator - **Mark Hawker**
Workshop Manager - **David Elliot**
Project Manager - **Sebastian Soper**
PR Manager - **Anne-Marie Clark (01752 230479)**

Box Office - **01752 267222**
www.theatreroyal.com

Registered Charity Number 284545

DIRECTOR'S NOTE
BETTER THAN BRECHT:
THE THEATRE OF ROLAND SCHIMMELPFENNIG

A British playwright sitting down to write this play might typically reach for his style from a relatively narrow spectrum on the formal bandwidth. You could try arguing similarly for the German playwright Roland Schimmelpfennig and say that his choices reach only back to Brecht and therefore into his own tradition. And there might be something in that: where we tend to be bound to naturalism and social realism by a variety of circumstances – the economy, flexibility and beauty of our language, with its GPS-like ability to place a character on a social and geographic grid being the main – German theatre has thrived on formal invention, an absolute necessity in their highly deconstructed theatre. And Schimmelpfennig is a prime example: a playwright with a background as dramaturg, someone who has therefore spent many years in rehearsal rooms watching actors and directors working on other people's plays and who understands and wants to challenge those processes. But the result is a highly intelligent, beautifully constructed and playful play. A piece that tackles a topical issue like migration but rather than hitting us over the head with the journalistic, transient rights and wrongs of the situation, takes us by the hand and leads us into a hall of mirrors where, with only our sense of empathy to navigate and distinguish, we piece together a poignant and important story for our global age, looking at the very deepest senses of the word 'journey'. Perhaps the fact that the play itself is a formal migrant to these shores adds power and piquancy to its impact.

As the incoming Artistic Director of Actors Touring Company, I'm thrilled to be opening my account with this play. I was lucky enough to be the first person to direct one of Roland's plays in England when I directed *Push Up* at the Royal Court in 2002 and the following year ATC presented another play of his, *Arabian Night*. But it isn't only the coincidence that makes this an important choice. I feel that this play carries within it the seeds of what ATC stands for: it's a play about the world today in the broadest sense, both in content and form, a play that powerfully restates the argument for theatre, a play that activates an audience and asks them not only to go on the journey with us but to help make that journey up. And it also playfully, wittily and movingly asks us to look at actors as humans and to see *all* the possibilities, both past, present and future that lie within them, be they age, gender or race. In that full act of seeing lies the chance for all of us to be expanded and humanized in a powerful, collective moment.

It gives me great pleasure to be opening this production in Plymouth, where the support of Simon Stokes and his team has allowed us to put together a tour that takes in the Traverse in Edinburgh, the Arcola in London and many other points along the way. I hope that in the years to come ATC will become synonymous with a theatre that stretches and rewards you, that brings you strange shapes and forms from other places and that always keeps the focus on the work of the actor and their relationship with you, the audience.

THE GOLDEN DRAGON

Roland Schimmelpfennig

THE GOLDEN DRAGON

translated by David Tushingham

OBERON BOOKS
LONDON

WWW.OBERONBOOKS.COM

First published in 2011 by Oberon Books Ltd
521 Caledonian Road, London N7 9RH
Tel: +44 (0) 20 7607 3637 / Fax: +44 (0) 20 7607 3629
e-mail: info@oberonbooks.com
www.oberonbooks.com

This translation was sponsored by Goethe-Institut

A catalogue record for this book is available from the British Library.

ISBN: 978-1-84943-124-8

Cover photography by Kendall O'Neill

Characters

A YOUNG MAN
(The Grandfather, Asian Man,
The Waitress, The Cricket)

A WOMAN OVER SIXTY
(The Granddaughter, Asian Woman,
The Ant, The Shopkeeper)

A YOUNG WOMAN
(The Man with the Striped Shirt,
Asian Man with Toothache, The Barbie-Fucker)

A MAN OVER SIXTY
(A Young Man, Asian Man, Second Stewardess)

A MAN
(The Woman in the Dress, Asian Man,
First Stewardess)

1.

THE MAN, THE WOMAN OVER SIXTY, THE YOUNG MAN, THE YOUNG WOMAN, THE MAN OVER SIXTY.

THE MAN: The Golden Dragon.

> Early evening.

> Pale summer light falls through the windows onto the tables. Five Asians in the tiny kitchen of the Thai/Chinese/Vietnamese fast food Restaurant.

THE YOUNG WOMAN: A young Chinese man, beside himself with toothache:

> *Beside herself.*

> It hurts, it hurts, it hurts –

> *THE YOUNG WOMAN screams with pain.*

THE YOUNG MAN: Don't cry, don't cry.

> *THE YOUNG WOMAN screams with pain.*

THE YOUNG WOMAN: It hurts –

THE WOMAN OVER SIXTY: He's in pain.

THE MAN OVER SIXTY: The boy's in pain.

THE YOUNG MAN: Don't cry – don't cry.

THE MAN: Don't scream, but he does scream; he screams, he's really screaming –

> *THE YOUNG WOMAN screams with pain.*

> *THE WOMAN OVER SIXTY fries noodles in a wok. It hisses.*

THE YOUNG WOMAN: It hurts so much – this tooth hurts so much –

THE MAN OVER SIXTY: We're standing round the boy in the tiny kitchen of the Chinese/Thai/Vietnamese restaurant.

> Don't scream, – he's really screaming.

THE WOMAN OVER SIXTY: Number 83: Pat Thai Gai: fried rice noodles with egg, vegetables, chicken and spicy peanut sauce, medium hot.

THE MAN: Toothache.

THE MAN OVER SIXTY: The boy's got toothache.

THE YOUNG WOMAN gasps with pain.

THE YOUNG MAN: Stir it, keep stirring.

THE WOMAN OVER SIXTY stirs the wok.

THE MAN OVER SIXTY: The boy.

THE YOUNG MAN: Out front two stewardesses sit down at a table by the window, table eleven. Hello.

THE YOUNG WOMAN gasps with pain.

THE MAN OVER SIXTY: Don't scream like that-

THE MAN: The first stewardess says:
    Hello.

THE MAN OVER SIXTY: The second stewardess says:
    Hello.

THE YOUNG MAN: Hello.

THE WOMAN OVER SIXTY: That tooth's got to come out.

THE YOUNG MAN: Can I get you some drinks?

THE YOUNG WOMAN: Oh God. My tooth, oh God. Oh God.

2.

THE YOUNG MAN and THE WOMAN OVER SIXTY.

THE YOUNG MAN: A mild evening in late summer. An old man with grey hair, very thin, haggard, sick maybe, stands on the balcony of his flat. His granddaughter has been visiting him, grandfather, grandad. She lives upstairs in the same building with her boyfriend in the little flat under the roof and now she was going to tell her grandfather something special, something very special, but she doesn't tell him because her grandfather seems lost in thought or worries.

Below them: the red lanterns of the Chinese/Thai/ Vietnamese restaurant THE GOLDEN DRAGON. Apparently everyone working in the kitchen is Vietnamese. But whether that's true –

The old man says:

If I could have one wish.

Pause.

If I could have one wish.

THE WOMAN OVER SIXTY: Next to the old man on the balcony a young woman, not yet nineteen. She is strikingly young and strikingly beautiful.

She says:

What is it, Grandad, what would you wish for?

THE YOUNG MAN: The old man looks at the young girl.

My granddaughter. I look at my granddaughter:

You –

Short Pause.

You're so young.

Short Pause.

You look wonderful.

THE WOMAN OVER SIXTY: You think so? Do you really think so, Grandad?

Pause.

When I get to be your age – what am I going to look like then –

THE YOUNG MAN: I'm not going to see that.

I'm not going to be around to see that.

I laugh.

He laughs or smiles.

THE WOMAN OVER SIXTY: You're laughing.

THE YOUNG MAN: I'll be dead a long time before then.

He laughs desperately.

I'll be dead and buried a long time before then.

THE WOMAN OVER SIXTY: But what was it, what were you going to say –

THE YOUNG MAN: What?

THE WOMAN OVER SIXTY: What you were going to say – you just said: If I could have one wish –

THE YOUNG MAN: Yes. I said that: if I could have one wish.

THE WOMAN OVER SIXTY: He pauses for a long time. Stands there with the empty wineglass in his hand. On the table are empty foil containers, number 101, Su ki ya ki, fried beef with straw mushrooms, bamboo shoots and glass noodles and number B6, the carrot curry, a Vietnamese speciality. I'd got them to take away, downstairs in THE GOLDEN DRAGON. He looks into the dusk.

Hm?

He says nothing. Then:

THE YOUNG MAN: And you? What would your wish be -

THE WOMAN OVER SIXTY: Yes, what – you've not said what you would wish for.

THE YOUNG MAN: Pause.

3.

*THE MAN, THE WOMAN OVER SIXTY, THE YOUNG MAN, THE YOUNG
WOMAN, THE MAN OVER SIXTY.*

THE MAN: In the kitchen of the Thai/Chinese/Vietnamese
restaurant THE GOLDEN DRAGON: it's cramped, it's very
cramped, there's no room, but there are still five Asian
cooks working here. One of them's got toothache: the boy,
the one who's looking for his sister. The new one.

THE YOUNG WOMAN screams in pain.

THE MAN OVER SIXTY: We call him the boy.

THE YOUNG WOMAN: It hurts –

THE WOMAN OVER SIXTY: Toothache.

THE YOUNG WOMAN: Oh that hurts, it really hurts.

THE MAN OVER SIXTY: Don't scream, don't scream -

THE MAN: Screaming will use up all your energy.

THE YOUNG MAN: We call him the boy because he's new.

THE WOMAN OVER SIXTY: Because he's not been here so
long. He's still new. And he's got no money. And he's got
no papers. So a dentist is out of the question.

Don't scream, don't scream so loud.

THE MAN: An apple juice. And a glass of white wine.

The drinks for the stewardesses.

THE MAN OVER SIXTY: That tooth's got to come out.

THE YOUNG WOMAN: How – how?

THE MAN: Get it out,

THE WOMAN OVER SIXTY: get it out,

THE YOUNG MAN: there's no other way.

THE WOMAN OVER SIXTY: Get it out, out –

4.

THE YOUNG WOMAN.

THE YOUNG WOMAN: The man in the striped shirt:

Late thirties maybe, already had a bit too much to drink. He's alone in his flat, sitting at the kitchen table. Looking at the table, the fridge. His girlfriend has left him, or she's thinking about leaving him and now he hopes she's going to come back.

He says: I wish she'd never met him.

If she hadn't met him –

A bit coarse. Rather desperate.

If she hadn't met him –

A sudden gesture. Which makes me knock some beer onto my trousers.

She spills some beer.

5.

THE MAN OVER SIXTY and THE WOMAN OVER SIXTY.

THE MAN OVER SIXTY: Two young people in the flat they share under the roof, lovers. They've only been living together a couple of months. A wonderful time, one they'll never forget. Downstairs: THE GOLDEN DRAGON. The young woman has just come back from seeing her grandfather, who lives in the same building. Her boyfriend, the young man, says:

How could it happen –

THE WOMAN OVER SIXTY: She goes: I don't know.

THE MAN OVER SIXTY: How could it happen –

THE WOMAN OVER SIXTY: I don't know how, I don't know how it happened –

THE MAN OVER SIXTY: I don't believe it – I do not believe it –

THE WOMAN OVER SIXTY: I have no idea –

THE MAN OVER SIXTY: You said –

THE WOMAN OVER SIXTY: Me?

THE MAN OVER SIXTY: You said nothing could happen –

THE WOMAN OVER SIXTY: Yes, that's right, I've no idea how it could have happened –

THE MAN OVER SIXTY: This is a complete disaster, a total disaster –

THE WOMAN OVER SIXTY cries.

THE MAN OVER SIXTY: Everything was going so well – it was all going well before – and now – how are we going to –

You're far too –

Short pause.

And the money – where are we going to –

Short pause.

The flat's too small for three – and in the Autumn you
were going to – you were planning to go to –
Short pause.
A total disaster.

6.

*THE MAN, THE WOMAN OVER SIXTY, THE YOUNG MAN, THE YOUNG
WOMAN, THE MAN OVER SIXTY.*

THE YOUNG MAN: In THE KITCHEN OF THE Thai/Chinese/
Vietnamese fast food restaurant THE GOLDEN DRAGON:

Hot woks, a gas stove, a deep fat fryer, a clock, a
Vietnamese calendar.

Liking the wrong things, liking things like sweets –
something he'd always done.

He'd done that at home.

THE MAN OVER SIXTY: Show me, show me your tooth – oh
God! It's completely black!

THE MAN: The stewardesses order: Twenty-five –

THE MAN OVER SIXTY: – and six.

THE YOUNG MAN: Twenty-five and six. Chinese noodle stir-fry
and the Thai soup.

THE MAN OVER SIXTY: Completely black!

THE YOUNG WOMAN: It really hurts –

THE YOUNG MAN: You've got to go to a dentist.

THE MAN OVER SIXTY: What dentist, how can he go to a
dentist –

THE MAN: One 31, two 17s, for the table in the corner and a 25
and a 6 for the women by the window, table eleven.

THE YOUNG MAN: Number 31: Gai Grob Prio Wan, crispy
chicken breast with straw mushrooms, pineapple and
peach in sweet and sour sauce.

THE MAN OVER SIXTY: Number 17: Bao-Zi (3 pieces), steamed
dumplings filled with pork and vegetables, made on the
premises!

THE WOMAN OVER SIXTY: Number 25: Bami Pat, fried egg
noodles with filet of chicken breast and fresh vegetables.

THE YOUNG WOMAN: Number 6: Thai soup with chicken, coconut milk, Thai ginger, tomatoes, button mushrooms, lemon grass and lemon leaves (hot).

7.

THE WOMAN OVER SIXTY. THE YOUNG MAN.

THE WOMAN OVER SIXTY: The ant diligently collected provisions all summer long, while his neighbour, the cricket, made music day and night.

She fiddled away day after day while the ant worked and worked, carrying the heaviest provisions into his burrow, while the song of the cricket wafted across the fields.

And then winter came. And the winter was cold. The frost came and the snow came. And the cricket could find nothing left to eat. She was starving. No music any more.

Finally the cricket went to the ant, where else could she go, and asked him for something to eat.

Can't you give me something to eat, please, I haven't eaten for days.

No answer.

Please, I'm so hungry.

No answer, and the ant avoids the cricket's eye.

The cricket looks terrible.

Please. Please, I need something to eat.

THE YOUNG MAN: Please. Please, I need something to eat.

THE WOMAN OVER SIXTY: Now the ant looks up.

I'm giving you nothing.

You didn't do a day's work all summer.

Not a single day.

I'm giving you nothing.

As far as I'm concerned you can starve.

You'll get nothing.

You'll get nothing from me.

8.

THE YOUNG WOMAN and THE MAN.

THE YOUNG WOMAN: In the kitchen of a four room apartment a couple of floors above the restaurant THE GOLDEN DRAGON. The man in the striped shirt, who spilt beer on his trousers and a woman in a red dress. In the corner, the silver fridge they bought together. Most of the things here are joint purchases, acquisitions for a shared future. Those weekend visits to the furniture and cutlery sections of department stores, in the early days, they didn't have much then, there was so much they didn't have, we need a corkscrew, we need a peppermill, we need a new frying pan, why, what's wrong with the old one, the old one's broken, we need some glasses, what do you think of this lamp, we need a salad bowl. She's come back:

Now you turn up!

says the man in the striped shirt.

Now! Now you're here! Well, it's too late now, it's too late! I don't want you now. I can't do this any more. I can't any more! I've waited and waited and waited, now it's too late –

He drinks.

She drinks.

If only you'd never met him!

Short pause.

Look at the state of me, I've spilt beer on my trousers and this shirt, this shirt, fucking stripes, I came straight from work, I came straight here, I was, of course I was hoping to see you here, we've got to wear this, everyone wears a suit and tie, yeah – that's it – that's the way it is – this is my life –

THE MAN: What do you think of my dress, the dress you –

Short pause.

I thought I'd wear it again, I wanted to – why can't we – go downstairs for something to eat, just go, we'll just keep going like nothing ever happened.

32

Short pause.

How are we going to –

Short pause.

do you want everything back, the earrings, the jewellery –

Short pause.

the ring? Do you want the ring back?

THE YOUNG WOMAN: The way you look, you look, the dress, in that dress, that dress that, you're stunning – stunning –

9.

THE YOUNG MAN.

THE YOUNG MAN: Hair, it'll go.

Teeth, they'll drop out.

When you're old: toothless, who'd have thought that your teeth really do drop out.

I so wish I could be the way I was once again. Young.

I wish I was young again.

Pause.

I would so love to be the way I was once.

10.

THE MAN, THE WOMAN OVER SIXTY, THE YOUNG MAN, THE YOUNG WOMAN, THE MAN OVER SIXTY.

THE MAN: Downstairs in THE GOLDEN DRAGON:

THE YOUNG MAN: Number 103: Twice-fried beef with bamboo shoots, onions, peppers, vegetables and garlic, hot.

THE YOUNG WOMAN screams.

THE MAN: Dish number 103 extra hot for the man from the shop next door to THE GOLDEN DRAGON, as always, to take away.

11.

THE WOMAN OVER SIXTY and THE MAN OVER SIXTY. She has bought children's toys.

THE MAN OVER SIXTY: What's that?

THE WOMAN OVER SIXTY: It's – it's a rattle.

THE MAN OVER SIXTY: A rattle –

Short pause.

THE WOMAN OVER SIXTY: And this is a toy clock.

Short pause.

THE MAN OVER SIXTY: Upstairs, in the little flat under the roof. The young couple who were having such a wonderful time until now in their first flat.

Short pause.

Why did you get all this?

THE WOMAN OVER SIXTY: So –

THE MAN OVER SIXTY: Why?

THE WOMAN OVER SIXTY: So you can get used to it.

Short pause.

So you'll be pleased.

THE MAN OVER SIXTY: But I'm not pleased.

Short pause.

I'm not pleased.

Short pause.

THE WOMAN OVER SIXTY: I got these things so it will be easier for you to start being pleased.

THE MAN OVER SIXTY: How am I supposed to start if I'm not pleased.

12.

THE WOMAN OVER SIXTY.

THE WOMAN OVER SIXTY: The ant says to the cricket:

You'll get nothing.

You'll get nothing from me.

If you want something, you'll have to work for it.

Brief pause.

But there's nothing you can do.

You haven't learnt anything.

13.

THE MAN, THE WOMAN OVER SIXTY, THE YOUNG MAN, THE YOUNG WOMAN, THE MAN OVER SIXTY.

THE MAN: In the back of the kitchen of the Thai/Chinese/ Vietnamese fast food restaurant THE GOLDEN DRAGON: Drink, drink something, some vodka.

THE YOUNG MAN: The boy has tears in his eyes.

THE YOUNG WOMAN: 30. 30 years old, born in Qingdao on the Yellow Sea, a long, long, long way from here.

THE MAN: Drink, drink something, some vodka.

THE MAN OVER SIXTY: The thin man pours vodka into the boy's open mouth.

THE WOMAN OVER SIXTY: Number 74: Bangkok-style Duck red curry with fresh mushrooms, peppers, bamboo shoots, onions, lemon grass and coconut (hot).

The little Chinese boy screams and screams, and he's not used to vodka.

THE YOUNG WOMAN: The toothache is unbearable.

THE YOUNG MAN: Number 51: Phad Med Mamoang Nüah; Beef in satay sauce with peppers, onions, carrots and cashew nuts.

DER MANN: He's going to pass out on us like this.

THE YOUNG MAN: He's going to pass out on us any minute.

THE WOMAN OVER SIXTY: That tooth's got to come out.

THE MAN OVER SIXTY: The tooth's got to come out! Out!

THE YOUNG WOMAN: It hurts, it hurts –

THE MAN OVER SIXTY: Under the small sink, everything's small, everything's cramped, everything's hot, there are five of us cooking in here,

THE MAN: Everything's cramped, a few square feet of tiling, twenty or thirty maybe, the gas cooker and the deep fat fryer, the work surfaces, the fridges, next door a little space for storage, a clock on the wall, from the Vietnamese wholesaler, I'd like to go to Vietnam, the coast is supposed to be wonderful.

THE WOMAN OVER SIXTY burns herself

Number 13: Satay Sticks, chicken in peanut sauce.

THE YOUNG WOMAN gasps in pain.

THE MAN OVER SIXTY: Under the sink:

THE MAN: Under the sink the toolbox:

THE YOUNG MAN: The toolbox, the red spanner, it's needed all the time for the gas cooker.

THE YOUNG WOMAN: Not the spanner, please not the spanner –

THE MAN OVER SIXTY: Don't be afraid, my friend, don't be afraid.

THE MAN: The fat man pours vodka over the spanner.

THE MAN OVER SIXTY: Open your mouth. Open your mouth –

THE YOUNG WOMAN: No!

THE MAN: I pour some more vodka in his mouth, that helps, it helps. Swallow it, swallow it –

THE MAN OVER SIXTY: Which one is it then, this one,

THE MAN: The fat man knocks on the tooth with the spanner.

THE MAN OVER SIXTY: or that one there – the right incisor – it's not looking good, or the left one, it's not looking good either!

THE MAN: The fat man knocks on the tooth with the spanner.

THE YOUNG WOMAN leaps up in pain.

THE MAN OVER SIXTY: They both look bad –

14.

THE MAN, eventually also THE WOMAN OVER SIXTY.

THE MAN: Next door to the GOLDEN DRAGON a little shop that's open late into the night, it's got everything, food, alcohol, tobacco. Everything you need. Noodles, oil, tins, cola, spices, rice, cheese, meat, ready meals, milk. Ice cream. Vegetables. Fruit. Yogurt. There are magazines, newspapers, lottery tickets. They've even got soap, toothpaste. Cleaning products. Nappies. Everyone can find what they're looking for here, they've got everything. The shop is so full, there's hardly room to move in the place.

The man who owns the shop, Hans, has gone and got a takeaway from the Golden Dragon:

Number 103, as always, or as usual: Twice-fried beef with bamboo shoots, onions, peppers, vegetables and garlic, hot.

Extra hot.

15.

THE WOMAN OVER SIXTY and THE YOUNG MAN.

THE WOMAN OVER SIXTY: The ant asks the cricket what she can do. Whether she can do anything special.

What can you do then? Dance, huh. Well dance then. Go on. Come on. Get on with it. Show me. Show me, then maybe you'll get something. You can dance for me.

The cricket dances.

Yeah, it's pretty, but what use is it.

What use is that to me. It's beautiful, the way you dance.

But I'm not really interested.

Not interested at all.

16.

THE MAN, THE WOMAN OVER SIXTY, THE YOUNG MAN, THE YOUNG WOMAN, THE MAN OVER SIXTY.

THE YOUNG MAN: In the Chinese/Thai/Vietnamese takeaway THE GOLDEN DRAGON.

> The old man takes a small wooden stick and probes inside the hole in the tooth.

THE MAN: The stick, a wooden stick like we use for number 13, satay sticks with peanut sauce, is inside the hole in the tooth.

> *THE YOUNG WOMAN screams or gasps.*

THE MAN OVER SIXTY: Completely hollow – that's the one –

THE WOMAN OVER SIXTY: Is that it?

THE MAN OVER SIXTY: That's it –

THE WOMAN OVER SIXTY: That one?

THE MAN OVER SIXTY: That one

> *THE MAN OVER SIXTY grabs the spanner and gets to work.*

THE MAN: Number 76: Gaeng Kiau Wan Pag: green curry with mixed vegetables and coconut with Thai basil.

> *THE YOUNG WOMAN screams.*

THE YOUNG MAN: Shh, shh, don't scream, don't scream, not so loud, it'll soon be over –

17.

THE WOMAN OVER SIXTY and THE YOUNG MAN

THE WOMAN OVER SIXTY: The ant makes the starving cricket some suggestions.

Cleaning. You can clean. If you want something, you've got to earn it.

What about cleaning.

Do some cleaning.

Or – that gives me an idea –

18.

THE MAN, THE WOMAN OVER SIXTY, THE YOUNG MAN, THE YOUNG WOMAN, THE MAN OVER SIXTY.

THE MAN OVER SIXTY: In the Thai/Chinese/Vietnamese restaurant THE GOLDEN DRAGON:

THE MAN: The Old Man tightens the spanner.

THE MAN OVER SIXTY: I tighten the spanner, it's not easy, because the boy is thrashing his head backwards and forwards all the time, backwards and forwards, backwards and forwards –

19.

THE WOMAN OVER SIXTY.

THE WOMAN OVER SIXTY: The ant rents the cricket out to other ants.

The ants lust after the cricket. They think she's vulgar, they think she's sexy, they're get off on her accent, as much as the cricket can speak the ants' language. They've already taught her what they think are the most important words. To the ants, the cricket is a dirty slapper. The ants do what they like with the cricket. They take her roughly. They fuck her ragged, frequently one after another. In exchange the cricket receives something to eat afterwards. Bits of dead flies. But sometimes she doesn't get anything. Then the ants say the cricket should be glad she's got a roof over her head. They say the cricket should be glad the ants don't send her away. Back. Back into the snow.

20.

THE MAN, THE WOMAN OVER SIXTY, THE YOUNG MAN, THE YOUNG WOMAN, THE MAN OVER SIXTY.

THE MAN OVER SIXTY: In the Thai/Chinese/Vietnamese restaurant THE GOLDEN DRAGON:

THE MAN: The old man tightens the spanner.

THE MAN OVER SIXTY: I tighten the spanner, it's not easy, because the boy's thrashing his head backwards and forwards all the time, backwards and forwards, backwards and forwards, watch it or I'll pull the wrong tooth out by mistake, a healthy one, but the thin one holds the boy, holds him tight, a bit more vodka,

THE MAN pours vodka into the Chinese boy's mouth.

THE WOMAN OVER SIXTY: Number B2, Bun Cha Gio Chay, Rice noodles, crispy fried spring rolls, salad, beansprouts, cucumber, roasted onions, peanuts, Vietnamese basil and coriander.

THE MAN: Be calm, boy, nice and calm,

THE YOUNG WOMAN: Don't, don't –

THE YOUNG MAN: He tightens the spanner,

THE WOMAN OVER SIXTY: Number 82: Pat Thai Gai, stir-fried rice noodles.

THE MAN OVER SIXTY: I tighten the spanner,

THE MAN: The boy screams. He can see the spanner –

THE WOMAN OVER SIXTY: We call him the boy.

THE YOUNG WOMAN: He snaps the tooth out of my mouth,

Long pause.

he snaps it off me,

Short pause.

He pulls it out of me –

THE YOUNG MAN: And the tooth flies through the air.

Pause.

THE MAN OVER SIXTY: I rip the tooth out of his mouth, his
right front tooth and the bloody, half-rotten tooth flies
through the air.

THE WOMAN OVER SIXTY: Up into the air –

THE YOUNG WOMAN: The tooth
flies and it flies and it keeps flying.

21.

THE MAN. THE YOUNG WOMAN.

THE MAN: The woman in the red dress has packed a few things. Only essential clothing, everything else is staying here, the joint purchases for a shared future. Corkscrew, pepper mill, the frying pan, the glasses, the lamp, the salad bowl. Her husband or her former husband was quite drunk by the end of their talk, and in the end he ran off to buy some more to drink in the little shop downstairs, beer, wine or vodka.

  The woman is in the kitchen.

  He hasn't come back. She won't wait much longer.

  It can't be –

  Short pause.

  It can't be that I married the wrong man.

  Short pause.

  It can't be that everything's falling apart.

  Short pause.

  And it's my fault.

  Short pause. Previously:

  I've met another man.

THE YOUNG WOMAN: You've done what?

THE MAN: I've met another man.

THE YOUNG WOMAN: That can't be –

THE MAN: It's true. It happened.

  Short pause.

  We just met.

  By chance.

THE YOUNG WOMAN: Where – Who – who –

THE MAN: We were rehearsing with the choir. He'd just joined –

  Good looking, sense of humour.

48

One time afterwards, after the rehearsal, he bought everyone drinks, later.

He was a good dancer. He was a very good dancer.

THE YOUNG WOMAN: You danced with him?

Pause.

THE MAN: Yes.

Short pause.

Yes I did.

Short pause.

I've fallen in love.

THE YOUNG WOMAN: And – and now – I –

THE MAN: I was never planning to leave my husband, never.

Only it kept getting stronger. It was too big.

Suddenly being with him seemed much bigger than everything my husband and I had ever experienced. It all paled.

THE YOUNG WOMAN: You lied to me.

THE MAN: And then: a secret weekend in Venice, and I lied,

I said I was with my best friend, with Eva, who I've known since primary school, when we both ran around with long plats. Eva is always away anyway, and she even lives here in the building, Eva covered for me. She lied for me. She said it was great in Venice.

Short pause.

And it was beautiful. Really beautiful.

22.

THE MAN, THE WOMAN OVER SIXTY, THE YOUNG MAN, THE YOUNG
WOMAN, THE MAN OVER SIXTY.

THE YOUNG WOMAN: The tooth flies and flies –

THE YOUNG MAN: flies and it flies –

THE MAN: It flies and it keeps flying through the tiny kitchen
of THE GOLDEN DRAGON –

THE MAN OVER SIXTY: The extracted tooth keeps on flying –

THE WOMAN OVER SIXTY: it keeps on flying and lands in the
wok.

Number 82: Pat Thai Gai, Stir-fried rice noodles,

What's that, what is that – you've got to be joking, you
know that, you have got to be joking.

THE MAN: She is 69 years old, born on the northern edge of
the Chinese highlands, far away, far away from here, now
she takes a large spoon and tries to fish the tooth out of the
wok,

THE YOUNG MAN: Still waiting for the soup, no. 6.

THE WOMAN OVER SIXTY: I want to get that tooth out of the
wok full of stir-fried rice noodles, number 82, I'm trying to
fish it out of the pan with a large spoon –

THE YOUNG MAN: Number six, Thai soup with chicken –

THE WOMAN OVER SIXTY: And the tooth shoots out of the
wok, it flies and keeps on flying till it lands in the soup
bowl, no. 6, Thai soup with chicken, coconut milk, Thai
ginger, tomatoes, button mushrooms, lemon grass and
lemon leaves, (hot)

number 6 is on its way with the thin, pretty one, 26, not
even fifty kilos, from the Gulf of Tongking, number 6, the
soup is on its way out, it's just being carried out,

THE YOUNG MAN: Table eleven, two women by the window,
twenty-eight and thirty-one, both in the dark blue uniforms

of flight attendants, one of them has dark brown hair, the other one is blonde, both of them come here a lot, they live together here in the building, they share a flat, and the dark one has a boyfriend who she brings with her sometimes,

the dark one had ordered number 25: Bami Pat, fried egg noodles with chicken breast and fresh vegetables and the other one number 6, the Thai soup with chicken, coconut milk, Thai ginger, tomatoes, button mushrooms, lemon grass and lemon leaves, (hot), they're both tired, they've both been on a long flight, they've come from Santiago de Chile, that's almost as far south as you can get, they've flown over the Andes, then they had a stop-over in Buenos Aires,

THE MAN: Buenos Aires is supposed to be wonderful,

THE YOUNG MAN: But they didn't have a chance to see the city,

THE MAN: And then they talk about things like suitcases with wheels on and uniforms and hair styles and people at work, the two of them share a flat, right here in the building, and they're both really tired,

THE YOUNG MAN: And the pretty waitress brings them their food, one 25. Number 25: Bami Pat, fried egg noodles with chicken breast and fresh vegetables, one number 6, Thai soup with chicken.

Long pause.

THE MAN: And then they eat in silence.

23.

THE WOMAN OVER SIXTY.

THE WOMAN OVER SIXTY: She's not a bad little girl, that one, have you, you've got to give it a try. She'll do anything. For something to eat, she'll do anything.

Short pause.

Anything.

Short pause.

I really do mean anything.

Short pause.

Anything.

Short pause.

Anything you want.

24.

THE MAN, THE WOMAN OVER SIXTY, THE YOUNG MAN, THE YOUNG WOMAN, THE MAN OVER SIXTY.

THE YOUNG MAN: It wasn't such a good idea, going for a meal together after such a long flight, what have you got left to say to each other, it would have been better if they'd gone straight to the flat, but this is what had been arranged, and somehow that stuck -

THE YOUNG WOMAN: But after an eighteen hour flight they don't have much left to say,

THE MAN OVER SIXTY: Nothing new, at any rate,

THE MAN: And the air in the plane –

The long flight –

THE WOMAN OVER SIXTY: The long flight across the Ocean, you can see on the screens how the plane creeps up the West coast of Africa at five hundred miles per hour.

THE MAN: And the air in the plane is terrible.

Whenever I fly across the Atlantic, I always think of sharks.

THE MAN OVER SIXTY: But when you look down out of the window, you don't see much.

THE MAN: Every seat on the flight has been taken. Chileans, Argentinians, Bolivians, with the faces of Indios,

THE YOUNG MAN: The meal is served, there's a choice of chicken fricassee or pasta.

THE MAN: And once they've flown past Angola, Gabon, Liberia and Sierra Leone and they've got as far as Gambia and Senegal and Mauritania, Inga, one of the stewardesses, says to Eva, the other one, look down there,

THE MAN OVER SIXTY: What is there?

THE MAN: Look there!

THE MAN OVER SIXTY: I can't see anything. What is it?

THE MAN: There, look –

THE MAN OVER SIXTY: I can't see anything, there's just water,

THE MAN: No, there –

THE MAN OVER SIXTY: Where?

THE MAN: There! Isn't that a boat?

THE MAN OVER SIXTY: A boat? How can you see that from here –

THE MAN: Yes, it's a boat! A boat full of people, can't you see it?

THE MAN OVER SIXTY: From thirty-three thousand feet up –

25.

THE YOUNG MAN.

THE YOUNG MAN: An old man came to the cricket and told her:

Do me.

Come on. Do me.

I want to be young again.

But it didn't work. The cricket did what she could, but he couldn't be young again, no matter what the cricket did.

If I could have one wish, said the old man.

And then for a long time he said nothing. And she did what she could. And he said nothing for a long time and then he got very angry.

The old man got very angry with himself, with old age, he got angry because he couldn't be young any more and in the end he got angry with the cricket.

I thought you knew what to do.

I thought you knew what to do.

And because the old man was so angry, he was unfair, and he was rough. Violent. He couldn't be young any more but he was still strong and heavy. And he tore out one of the cricket's feelers.

26.

THE MAN, THE WOMAN OVER SIXTY, THE YOUNG MAN, THE YOUNG WOMAN, THE MAN OVER SIXTY.

THE MAN OVER SIXTY: Now Inga and Eva, the two stewardesses, are eating, number 25 and number 6, and the conversation picks up again briefly, because they're talking about the sunset when flying West, they talk about nightfall above cloud level, the end of the day being distorted, teased out into something strange and long, and they talk about the sunrise when flying East, they talk about daybreak above cloud level, red and unreal, a sunrise which the plane is flying towards, a dawn which is distorted, stunted, squeezed, and how beautiful it is nevertheless.

THE MAN: Then they're both silent again, this time for a long time, both thinking, sometimes their eye falls on the carpet on the wall, which shows a golden dragon, the waitress asks:

Would you like any more drinks?

THE YOUNG MAN: Would you like any more drinks?

THE MAN OVER SIXTY: No, thank you.

THE YOUNG MAN: Smile, all three smile,

THE MAN: The girl, the waitress, 26, from the Gulf of Tongking, and one stewardess, Eva, dark hair, 28, and the other stewardess, Inga, blonde, 31, all three smile, the waitress walks past,

THE MAN OVER SIXTY: The dark stewardess, Eva, carries on eating her 25, Bami Pat and Inga, the blonde stewardess, eats number 6, the Thai soup,

THE MAN: Would you like to try this, Eva -

THE MAN OVER SIXTY: Yeah, sure, Inga –

THE MAN lets THE MAN OVER SIXTY try the soup.

THE MAN: She slurps the soup off the spoon,

THE MAN OVER SIXTY: Eva slurps the soup off the spoon.

The best Asian soup I ever had was in San Francisco,

THE MAN: Yes?

THE MAN OVER SIXTY: Yes, in San Francisco. Wonderful – it's really good, wonderful,

THE MAN: It is, isn't it,

and then in the bottom of the soup bowl in among the lemon grass and the Thai ginger and the tomatoes and the button mushrooms Inga finds a tooth, a bloody tooth.

Lying in the bottom of the bowl,

the tooth,

a tooth, an entire tooth, slightly bloodied, decayed,

a human incisor,

that's disgusting, says the dark one,

I'm not eating any more.

THE MAN OVER SIXTY: A human incisor,

that's disgusting, I'm not eating any more, we're leaving,

I'm leaving, I'm not staying here a minute longer,

disgusting, that is disgusting,

a tooth, a bloody tooth in the soup,

are you coming? You're not coming?

Stands up, walks, storms out.

THE MAN: The blonde woman, Inga, thirty-one, stays sitting there, with the tooth with a gruesome hole in it on the spoon in front of her. She keeps looking at the tooth.

THE WOMAN OVER SIXTY: Other people find a golden ring in the stomach of a fish.

THE MAN OVER SIXTY: Other people find a diamond in long grass.

27.

THE MAN, THE WOMAN OVER SIXTY, THE YOUNG MAN, THE YOUNG WOMAN, THE MAN OVER SIXTY.

THE MAN: In the kitchen of the Asian/Thai/Vietnamese restaurant THE GOLDEN DRAGON the hole where the boy's tooth was will not stop bleeding.

THE YOUNG WOMAN: It's really bleeding.

THE MAN OVER SIXTY: Let me have another look -

THE YOUNG WOMAN: It's been bleeding the whole time.

THE WOMAN OVER SIXTY: Show me – we have to singe it, maybe we have to singe it, so it stops bleeding –

THE MAN: Where's the tooth, the tooth, what if we just put the tooth back in the hole -

THE YOUNG MAN: The tooth's gone.

THE MAN: Gone?

THE YOUNG MAN: Gone.

THE MAN OVER SIXTY: Where's the tooth –

THE MAN: Where's it got to, it must be somewhere – didn't it drop on the floor, it must have –

28.

THE MAN.

THE MAN: Inside the handbag of a blonde woman around thirty, at night on the way up the stairs into her flat. A lipstick, a door key, make up, aspirin, tampons, a pen. A telephone. A little address book. Handkerchiefs. Old cinema tickets, Japanese matches, cigarettes. A receipt: cardigan. A cheap pair of sunglasses from Chile. Wrapped in a red paper napkin, one human incisor, severely decayed.

29.

THE MAN, THE WOMAN OVER SIXTY, THE YOUNG MAN, THE YOUNG WOMAN, THE MAN OVER SIXTY.

THE MAN: The boy puts his head back and the old man tries to plug the hole in his upper jaw. The old man says: what is that –

THE MAN OVER SIXTY: What is that?

THE YOUNG MAN: B3: Heo Xao Xa O't, Vietnamese speciality, fried pork marinated in lemon grass with pineapple, tomatoes, Vietnamese mushrooms, bamboo shoots, onions, garlic and sesame with steamed rice.

THE MAN OVER SIXTY: I don't believe it.

THE YOUNG WOMAN: What?

THE MAN OVER SIXTY: I cannot believe this.

THE YOUNG WOMAN: What?

THE MAN OVER SIXTY: There's someone there –

THE YOUNG WOMAN: What?

THE MAN OVER SIXTY: There's someone inside –

THE MAN: Where?

THE MAN OVER SIXTY: In the hole!

30.

THE YOUNG WOMAN and THE WOMAN OVER SIXTY.

THE YOUNG WOMAN: In the shop next door to the restaurant.
The man in the striped shirt and the trousers soaked in
beer has stayed, he opened the bottle of vodka while he
was still in the shop and now he's standing at the counter
next to the scales and the little shop's cash register and he's
drinking with the owner, Hans.

THE WOMAN OVER SIXTY: Hans is saying, then leave her,
leave her.

Then leave her, leave her. You know, you know,

Hans like the man in the striped shirt has already had quite
a few,

you know the saying, don't you:

THE YOUNG WOMAN: No, I don't know it.

THE WOMAN OVER SIXTY: It's something like: it's not worth
upsetting yourself over women.

Or: Never let a woman get you down.

Or: no woman is worth getting all miserable about.

I don't know either. I can't really remember.

In the foil container under the counter, the smell still hangs
in the room, the leftovers of number 103. Twice-fried beef,
with bamboo shoots, onions, peppers, vegetables and
garlic, hot.

Anyway I've got something special for you. Maybe. Come
with me.

THE YOUNG WOMAN: Hans locks the shop from the inside.
He pulls open a drawer behind his heavy shop counter, at
first sight it's full of rubber bands and screws and takes out
a key.

Come with me.

Let's see, maybe, maybe. You're my friend. Come with me.

31.

THE YOUNG MAN.

THE YOUNG MAN: The cricket waits in the ant's dark burrow for winter to end. She waits and waits but she's lost all sense of time since she can't see the sun any more, she can't say how long she's been here. Sometimes she thinks: maybe winter was over ages ago. Maybe outside it's summer again.

SCHIMMELPFENNIG / TUSHINGHAM

32.

THE MAN, THE WOMAN OVER SIXTY, THE YOUNG MAN, THE YOUNG WOMAN, THE MAN OVER SIXTY.

THE WOMAN OVER SIXTY: In THE GOLDEN DRAGON, number 41, Thai Chicken, crispy baked filet of chicken breast with ginger, beans, beansprouts, bamboo shoots, lemon leaves, lemon grass and red curry sauce (very hot)

THE MAN OVER SIXTY: I don't believe it.

THE YOUNG WOMAN: What?

THE MAN OVER SIXTY: I cannot believe this.

THE YOUNG WOMAN: What?

THE MAN OVER SIXTY: There's someone there –

THE YOUNG WOMAN: What?

THE MAN OVER SIXTY: There's someone inside –

In the hole where the young Chinese boy's tooth was, a group of people are sitting in a circle.

THE MAN: Why do you never call? You should call us. We've been waiting so long for you to phone.

THE YOUNG WOMAN: In the hole where the tooth was, which has not stopped bleeding, sit my mother, my father, my uncle, my aunt and a couple more people.

Why do you never call? You should call us.

THE WOMAN OVER SIXTY: I'm worried, says the mother.

I'd at least like to know whether you got there.

THE YOUNG WOMAN: And my father says: I'd at least like to know, where you are, my son.

THE MAN OVER SIXTY: Where are you, my son?

THE YOUNG WOMAN: I'm in THE GOLDEN DRAGON, in the kitchen, and Uncle has pulled out one of my teeth.

THE MAN: A tooth, that's terrible! Tell us –

THE YOUNG WOMAN: Yes, it's terrible –

THE MAN: Tell us, are you earning well,

THE YOUNG WOMAN: I know, Uncle, I know, you'll get it all back,

THE YOUNG MAN: And what about your sister? Have you found your sister yet?

THE YOUNG WOMAN: I've got to go now, all the best, good bye.

THE MAN OVER SIXTY: Good bye, my boy, and look after yourself. Have you found your sister yet?

THE YOUNG WOMAN: No I've not found her yet, but I don't know where I'm supposed to look –

THE WOMAN OVER SIXTY: Look after yourself, boy, look after yourself, how was the journey?

THE YOUNG WOMAN: I've got to go, I'm sorry, it's bleeding so much, good bye, the journey, yes well, another time maybe, good bye.

THE MAN OVER SIXTY: Good bye, boy, and look after yourself.

33.

THE MAN OVER SIXTY.

THE MAN OVER SIXTY: A young man approached the ant and said: you've got that cricket in your flat. What does she cost for an hour?

A short time later the young man was alone with the little cricket in a room. There wasn't much there, just a bed, a table, a chair.

You know, he said, my girlfriend's pregnant, and I didn't want the child, and since she's been pregnant I can't touch her any more, I find it repulsive. And then I had to find a new job because otherwise there wouldn't be enough money for three, now I have to feed everyone, and I think I deserve something for myself, I think I deserve something really special and now I'm going to let myself have it. And then he treated the cricket not like a cricket, but like a thing, that can be paid for and that doesn't matter if it gets broken. He probably treated the cricket the way he would have liked to have treated his pregnant girlfriend.

And when the ant saw what the young man had done to the cricket, he said: You can't come back, or: you can come back, but for what you want, you've got to pay a lot more: three times as much.

34.

THE MAN.

THE MAN: Night, in the two stewardesses' flat.

Inga, the blonde stewardess, sits at the table alone in the dark. The only light comes from the streetlamp outside. She has yet to take off her uniform, the dark blue skirt, the tights, the high-heeled shoes. The scarf.

Lying in front of her in the light of the streetlamp is the tooth.

The tooth has a hole in it. It lies on the table in front of her. The hole runs through the entire tooth, an incisor, it's possible to see right through the hole.

She's still wearing her uniform. Her tights, her skirt. Normally, whenever she gets home after such a long flight she gets undressed straight away. Her tights, her shoes.

How did the tooth get into the soup? Number 6, Thai soup with chicken, coconut milk, Thai ginger (hot), who did the tooth belong to? How much pain did that person the tooth belong to, feel?

She calls out to her flatmate, Eva.

Eva?

But Eva doesn't hear her, she's in the next room, her boyfriend's there.

The tooth lies on the table in front of the blonde woman.

The woman puts the tooth in her mouth.

THE MAN puts the tooth in his mouth.

The tooth tastes a little bit like the Thai soup and it tastes a little bit like blood.

Her tongue feels for the hole in the strange tooth.

His tongue feels for the hole in the strange tooth.

And then the blonde stewardess puts the tooth back on the table.

What is she going to do with the tooth? She can't throw it away.

35.

THE YOUNG WOMAN and THE WOMAN OVER SIXTY.

THE YOUNG WOMAN: The shopkeeper lives above his shop, you only have to go up one flight of stairs. The man in the striped shirt says:

I've never been inside your flat.

THE WOMAN OVER SIXTY: The shopkeeper says:

You've never been inside my flat?

THE YOUNG WOMAN: No –

THE WOMAN OVER SIXTY: Really?

THE YOUNG WOMAN: No! Never!

THE WOMAN OVER SIXTY stops for a moment.

Come in, come in –

THE YOUNG WOMAN: This is –

THE WOMAN OVER SIXTY: What –

THE YOUNG WOMAN: This is incredible –

THE WOMAN OVER SIXTY: Why –

THE YOUNG WOMAN: The man in the striped shirt opens another beer and walks incredulously around in the shopkeeper's flat –

This is incredible –

THE WOMAN OVER SIXTY: Why, what is –

THE YOUNG WOMAN: The shopkeeper's flat is not a flat, but rather a kind of warehouse, which is stacked to the roof with provisions. Rice, noodles, UHT milk, salt, sugar, all over the place, everywhere's full. Dried fish, meat.

This, this isn't a flat,

THE WOMAN OVER SIXTY: Why?

THE YOUNG WOMAN: It's a warehouse –

THE WOMAN OVER SIXTY: A warehouse, what kind of warehouse?

THE YOUNG WOMAN: A warehouse for provisions, everything here's full.

THE WOMAN OVER SIXTY: Provisions are important – provisions are more than important, in summer nobody thinks about them, but in the winter, when it gets cold...

THE YOUNG WOMAN: You're going to have to dig a tunnel to get through that lot.

Drinks. The shopkeeper drinks too.

36.

THE MAN, THE YOUNG WOMAN, THE MAN OVER SIXTY.

THE MAN: Inga, the stewardess, at the table at night, with no light. The only light the glow of the streetlamp. In front of her: the tooth on the table, the tooth casts a shadow.

What to do with it, I can't throw it away, but I can't keep it either.

In the next room, Eva, the second stewardess, says to her boyfriend:

THE MAN OVER SIXTY: You know what, downstairs in THE GOLDEN DRAGON tonight Inga found a tooth in her soup.

THE YOUNG WOMAN: What kind of soup –

THE MAN OVER SIXTY: In the Chinese downstairs, the Thai soup, number 6. A human tooth.

THE YOUNG WOMAN: I've never found a tooth in my soup.

THE MAN OVER SIXTY: When Eva and her boyfriend met, he told her, you look like a Barbie doll,

THE YOUNG WOMAN: You look like a Barbie doll.

THE MAN OVER SIXTY: And when they got together, she told him: now you're the Barbie-fucker.

Now you're the Barbie-fucker.

THE YOUNG WOMAN laughs

Yeah, I'm the Barbie fucker.

Short pause.

How was the flight?

THE MAN OVER SIXTY: How was the flight, the Barbie-fucker asks now.

The flight was ok, everything was fine until Inga found a tooth in her soup.

THE YOUNG WOMAN: Shall we go to bed?

THE MAN: Eva next door in bed with her boyfriend who she calls the Barbie-fucker.

In the dark living room on the table in front of the blonde woman: the tooth.

37.

THE YOUNG MAN, THE WOMAN OVER SIXTY.

THE WOMAN OVER SIXTY: It's getting late. The granddaughter rings on her grandfather's bell. Grandfather, there was something else I wanted to tell you.

THE YOUNG MAN: Yes, what is it, my child? What is it, what's the matter?

Short pause.

What's the matter?

THE WOMAN OVER SIXTY: I'm going to have a baby.

THE YOUNG MAN: A baby –

Short pause.

So?

THE WOMAN OVER SIXTY: I'm going to have a baby but I don't want to. I wish everything was like it was before.

38.

THE YOUNG MAN.

THE YOUNG MAN: The cricket in the little room in the ant's burrow, there's not much here, a chair, a table, a bed.

Sometimes she thinks winter must have been over ages ago, she wants to see if it's not already summer.

But she's afraid, that something will happen to her on the way. That she won't get out in one piece.

39.

THE MAN, THE WOMAN OVER SIXTY, THE YOUNG MAN, THE YOUNG WOMAN, THE MAN OVER SIXTY.

THE MAN: In the Thai/Chinese/Vietnamese restaurant THE GOLDEN DRAGON.

The boy will not stop bleeding.

THE YOUNG MAN: If we could find the tooth!

THE WOMAN OVER SIXTY: The tooth's gone.

THE MAN: Number 30: Bami Goreng – fried noodles with chicken, shrimps, curry and vegetables (Medium hot).

THE YOUNG WOMAN: I'm really cold.

THE MAN OVER SIXTY: He's really pale.

THE YOUNG WOMAN: So cold, but it's always warm in here.

THE WOMAN OVER SIXTY: Warm, it's warm, yes, from the gas rings, it's warm here –

THE YOUNG WOMAN: It's cold here.

THE MAN: It's your circulation.

THE MAN OVER SIXTY: Did you talk to your mum! Through the hole in your mouth!

THE YOUNG MAN: Yeah, that's right, your circulation.

THE MAN OVER SIXTY: You ought to call her more often!

THE MAN: Number 71: Ra Pra, served on a hot iron skillet: squid with garlic, fresh chilli, vegetables and Thai basil.

And then the boy falls off his stool.

THE MAN OVER SIXTY: Hey, hey -

THE MAN: Hey, hey –

THE YOUNG MAN: Hey –

THE MAN: What's the matter, what's wrong with you –

40.

THE YOUNG WOMAN.

THE YOUNG WOMAN: Night in the shopkeeper Hans's flat: the shopkeeper and the man in the striped shirt, who today has separated permanently from his wife, who met another man at a choir rehearsal.

They are listening to very loud music, it's very loud, and they are almost completely drunk. Almost completely.

The music is so loud, it's throbbing in my ears.

The flat is dark, as if the windows have been covered, but the windows have not been covered, there's just shelving in front of them, everywhere, and the shelves are full of stuff, shelves and cupboards, all full of provisions, noodles, rice, sugar, salt. And in between all these shelves and cupboards there are two sofas, there is a single reading lamp on in one corner of the room.

They sit on the sofas, and they're so drunk they can hardly move.

41.

THE MAN, THE WOMAN OVER SIXTY, THE YOUNG MAN, THE YOUNG WOMAN, THE MAN OVER SIXTY.

THE WOMAN OVER SIXTY: In the kitchen of the Thai/Chinese/Vietnamese restaurant THE GOLDEN DRAGON:

Short pause.

The boy is white as snow –

THE MAN: White like a lily –

THE YOUNG MAN: White like cherry blossom.

THE MAN OVER SIXTY: He's dead.

THE WOMAN OVER SIXTY: He's bled to death.

Oh, poor boy, oh, poor boy.

THE MAN: Number B 5: Bo Xao Xa ot, fried beef with Chinese leaf, peppers, Vietnamese mushrooms, bamboo shoots, onions, garlic and lemon grass.

THE YOUNG WOMAN: The Chinese boy has bled to death and he's lying next to the red and blue gas bottles on the floor of the tiny kitchen of the Chinese/Thai/Vietnamese restaurant THE GOLDEN DRAGON.

42.

THE YOUNG MAN.

THE YOUNG MAN: The cricket in the little room in the ant's burrow, there's not much here, a chair, a table, a bed.

Sometimes she thinks winter must have been over ages ago, she wants to see if it's not already summer. But she's afraid that something will happen to her on the way. That she won't get out in one piece.

43.

THE MAN OVER SIXTY AND THE YOUNG WOMAN, WHO STANDS NEXT TO HIM..

THE MAN OVER SIXTY: Eva, the dark-haired flight attendant, and her boyfriend.

I've always called him the Barbie-fucker and in the beginning he maybe thought it was funny, and then he didn't think it was so funny any more, and then he thought it was funny again.

I know it's a stupid word, Barbie-fucker, and I don't know why I didn't stop calling him it.

I'm too young for him. I wonder what he feels when he touches my young body. When I touch his body I can feel the age. He's good looking, he's an attractive man. But I can feel the age of his skin. I like him a lot, but maybe I despise him at the same time. Or I despise myself and that's why I call him that.

Short pause.

If I could be something completely different from what I am.

If I could be something completely different from what I have to be. Another person.

Short pause.

If I could have one wish.

If I wasn't the flight attendant and the Barbie-fucker's lover any more. And if the Barbie-fucker wasn't the Barbie-fucker any more. If we could swap, then I'd be the still attractive pilot who's flown across every border to every country on earth and he – he would be the pretty flight attendant who is currently spending her life in a droning cylinder 33,000 feet above sea level handing out meals.

What would that be like –

44.

THE MAN, THE WOMAN OVER SIXTY, THE YOUNG MAN, THE YOUNG WOMAN, THE MAN OVER SIXTY.

THE MAN OVER SIXTY: In the kitchen of THE GOLDEN DRAGON the Chinese boy, the new one, who was looking for his sister or had looked for her, lies dead on the floor next to the gas bottles. Bled to death, quick as a flash.

THE WOMAN OVER SIXTY: What are we going to do with him –

THE YOUNG MAN: He can't –

THE MAN: He can't stay here –

THE MAN OVER SIXTY: He can't stay lying down there.

THE WOMAN OVER SIXTY: Oh, my boy, my boy –

THE YOUNG WOMAN: They wrap the dead Chinese boy in a carpet, which they took off the wall out front in the GOLDEN DRAGON, in a moment when there was no-one else in the restaurant.

It's the carpet with the golden dragon, which the dead Chinese boy always wanted to have a closer look at, because there aren't any carpets like that where he comes from. And now it's too late.

THE WOMAN OVER SIXTY: Oh, my boy, my boy.

THE YOUNG WOMAN: THE GOLDEN DRAGON closes. The light goes off in the restaurant, and the neon sign and the red lanterns go off outside the door. The click of the light switch.

One of the cooks locks the door from the outside.

The others leave the restaurant by the back way.

On their shoulders they are carrying a heavy rolled-up carpet.

It's a warm night.

45.

THE YOUNG MAN, THE YOUNG WOMAN, THE WOMAN OVER SIXTY.

THE YOUNG MAN: The cricket had thought that the ant had fallen asleep despite all the noise because they'd drunk so much, that's why she came out of the room at half past one in the morning. But the ant hadn't fallen asleep, he was awake or almost awake still, and he had a visitor, a man in a striped shirt, he was awake, they were both sitting there, drinking and smoking, and the music was so loud it was almost unbearable –

THE YOUNG WOMAN: Suddenly there's a young Asian girl standing in the room.

Pause.

Suddenly there's a young Asian girl standing in the room.

I say:

Hey, where did you come from?

THE YOUNG MAN: He says, hey, where did you come from?

THE YOUNG WOMAN: Hey, where, where, where did you come from, hey, Hans, where did she come from, Hans, Hans, wake up, look who's here, Hans, where did you get her from? Hans has fallen asleep. Hans, wake up, look, look who's here.

THE YOUNG MAN: The man in the striped shirt tells the cricket how beautiful she is. Come here, he says, sit down here.

He's completely drunk and there's something injured, rough, malevolent in his drunken look, a look the cricket already knows.

THE YOUNG WOMAN: No, no, no, Hans, wake up, hey, you look, you look like – you don't need to be afraid, honestly, there's no need to be afraid at all, look, I'm sitting here with Hans, with my friend Hans, and we've had a bit to drink, well, there's no law against it, but honestly, sweetheart,

I accidentally spill some beer,

She spills some beer.

THE YOUNG MAN: He accidentally spills some beer, not so bad, I clean it later,

THE YOUNG WOMAN: What did you say, what did you say?

THE YOUNG MAN: Not so bad, I clean it later –

THE YOUNG WOMAN: But there's no need to be afraid at all, don't be afraid, not of me! Not of me!

Short pause.

You look – you look so beautiful, with those thin arms and legs, you look, you look like –

You know what you look like, you look like a grasshopper.

Short pause.

You look like a Chinese grasshopper. Amazing. What a vision, in the middle of the night. Suddenly a whole foreign continent is standing in the room.

You bring thousands of years of history with you!

History, you understand?

China. The Great Wall. The Forbidden City. The desert. The Yellow River. The Silk Road. The invention of gunpowder and the printing press. That's all China. One billion Chinese.

Short pause.

That's where you're from. Isn't it? You do come from China?

Short pause.

Come here. Sit down. Come on, let's have a chat. Come here.

46.

THE MAN, THE WOMAN OVER SIXTY, THE YOUNG MAN, THE YOUNG WOMAN, THE MAN OVER SIXTY.

THE WOMAN OVER SIXTY: Night in the city, outdoors. On a bridge over a river. The four Asians from THE GOLDEN DRAGON and the dead young man rolled up in the carpet which used to hang out front in their restaurant.

You really want to throw him in the water?

THE MAN: Where else can we take him?

THE WOMAN OVER SIXTY: I don't know, somewhere, this isn't right.

THE MAN OVER SIXTY: Are we supposed to just leave him lying somewhere, are we supposed to just leave him lying somewhere in the street...

THE YOUNG WOMAN: I hope they're not going to throw me off the bridge, I'm wondering what it's like to fall off this bridge.

THE MAN: No, don't leave him lying in the street, what's going to happen to him if we leave him lying in the street –

THE WOMAN OVER SIXTY: Poor boy -

THE YOUNG WOMAN: I hope they're not going to throw me off the bridge.

THE MAN: Let's just throw him off the bridge –

THE MAN OVER SIXTY: Off the bridge?

THE MAN: Yes, we'll throw him off the bridge –

THE YOUNG WOMAN: They heave the carpet up onto the railing of the bridge, they have to turn it round again, and then they unroll it.

There it is again, the golden dragon, if only I could have looked at it earlier, I always wanted to get a good look at it, I can almost reach out after it, now the carpet flutters briefly in the wind.

Farewell.

I fall from the bridge into the water, my head plunges into the cold river, water rushes inside me through the hole left by the tooth and I swim for home.

The river picks me up and carries me along, mile after mile. It flushes me into the North Sea, a current carries me northwards, past Norway and then Finland and Russia into the icy Arctic Sea and if the sea is frozen over, I move along underneath the ice, maybe a fish is pulling me or a whale.

Past the whole of Russia, the whole of Siberia, I carry on moving through the Arctic Sea, it's a long journey.

I cross the Bering Straits and the Bering Sea.

And then comes the Kamchatka peninsula –

not far now, soon I'll be home.

Past Japan in the distance in the grey light of dawn and shortly before evening that same day, finally: China.

I'm there, I'm almost home. Only another 1800 miles up the Yellow River, upstream along the Huang He, upstream along the Yellow River, through three provinces, first West, and then North, and then I'm home.

But what do I look like? How long was I travelling for? Weeks? Months? Or years? It was a long journey. It was a very long journey. I could have been years I was travelling for.

What do I look like? No flesh left on my bones washed clean by the salt water and the river water. A few algae. Maybe not a pretty sight.

I'm happy to be back home again.

I'm hungry.

Hello, dear honoured uncle, I'm sorry, all the money, all those notes, everything you all contributed, you'll never see it again.

No, you'll never see it again, I'm sorry.

But I did the return trip for nothing, nothing at all, and all on my own.

Dear mother, how white your dark hair has become.

And father died two years ago? How sad.

My sister –

No, I didn't find my sister, I'm sorry, it wasn't easy, didn't she come back ages ago? I don't know what happened to her, I don't know, how could I find the girl, who knows where she is, and who she's with and what she has to do there for her money.

Maybe someone's taken her in, it might be a good sign that she's not been in touch, maybe she's cleaning somewhere, or she's dancing, has she never called? Maybe she can't call, maybe where she is right now there's no telephone. Maybe. Perhaps she's saving her money and would prefer not to call. She'd rather save up, for later. Maybe she'll be in touch soon.

I always had the feeling she was really close by. Perhaps she's well.

How am I? – Fine. Alright. It was a long way. I lost a tooth. It hurt right from the start, it started hurting just after we set off. And I thought it would be ok.

But it didn't get any better, the tooth kept hurting more and more. And it kept hurting till they took it out, in the Golden Dragon, in the kitchen in the back with a red spanner.

47.

THE WOMAN OVER SIXTY AND THE YOUNG WOMAN AND THE YOUNG MAN.

THE WOMAN OVER SIXTY: In the shopkeeper Hans's flat. Hans had just been asleep on the sofa:

Are you mad, look what you've done to her, look, look at that, the way she's bleeding, Oh God, Oh my God, she's not an animal!

THE YOUNG WOMAN: The man in the striped shirt, muted, not sober, he's not really interested:

Sorry, I'm sorry.

Sorry, I'm sorry.

Short pause.

THE WOMAN OVER SIXTY: Oh God – what did you do to her – this is –

THE YOUNG WOMAN: Yeah, sorry, I'm sorry. It just happened. Sorry.

THE WOMAN OVER SIXTY: How is she ever going to – how's she supposed to – are you drunk or something, you've completely ruined her, completely ruined –

Listen, my boy, you're going to pay for this, you can't just, you are going to pay me for this, the poor thing –

The shopkeeper cries.

THE WOMAN OVER SIXTY cries.

48.

THE MAN.

THE MAN: Inga, the blonde flight attendant, in her flat.

> She takes the tooth off the table, puts it in her jacket pocket and leaves the flat. Loud music throbs from the door of the first floor flat. That's the shopkeeper's flat.
>
> Not a soul on the streets.
>
> The city at night.
>
> The lights in the windows. Not much traffic.
>
> She's soon on the bridge over the river. The Chinese come towards her, or are they Vietnamese, the whole family, if they actually are a family, from the GOLDEN DRAGON.
>
> Good evening.

THE WOMAN OVER SIXTY: Good evening.

THE MAN: Good evening. Still up at this time?

THE MAN OVER SIXTY: Yes, yes, going for a bit of a walk.

THE YOUNG MAN: Politely: And you, still up, now, at this time? It's late.

THE MAN: Yes, it's late. But I'm not tired.

THE WOMAN OVER SIXTY: Not tired!

THE MAN: No, I'm not tired.

> Inga could now say, look, I found this tooth in my soup today, in the Thai soup, No. 6 Thai soup with chicken, coconut milk, Thai ginger, tomatoes, button mushrooms, lemon grass and lemon leaves (hot) in your restaurant THE GOLDEN DRAGON, but she doesn't say this.

THE MAN OVER SIXTY: Yes, well, have a nice evening –

THE MAN: Yes, thanks, you too, good night.

THE WOMAN OVER SIXTY: Good night.

THE MAN: The blonde woman on the bridge.

The Chinese people have disappeared. She stops in the middle of the bridge and looks down into the black water.

She takes the tooth out of the jacket pocket of her stewardess uniform.

She puts it back in her mouth again.

Now it no longer tastes of blood and no longer of Thai soup.

The woman on the bridge spits the tooth out, like a cherry stone, I spit the tooth into the river.

Short pause.

The tooth in the air, briefly.

But then the darkness under the bridge swallows the tooth, the woman can neither see nor hear it fall into the water.

No-one apart from the blonde woman knows that from now on there is a tooth lying on the bed of the river. The tooth has gone. As if it had never been there.

Short pause. He puts a tooth in his mouth, and then spits it out. The tooth disappears into the darkness.

THE END